How Can We Describe Weather and Seasons?

HOUGHTON MIFFLIN HARCOURT

windy

snowy

Weather is what the air outside is like.
Weather can be sunny, snowy, rainy, or windy.

How do we know what the weather is like?

sunny

Monday

cloudy

Tuesday

rainy

Wednesday

The weather can change from day to day. Sometimes it changes in one day.

air moving a little

air moving a lot

Wind is moving air.
A windsock can tell us about the wind.

What can a windsock tell us?

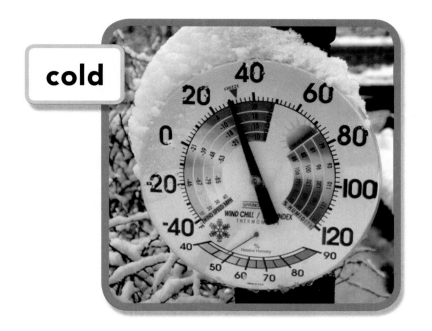

cold

Air can be warm or cold.
A thermometer tells how warm
or cold the air is.

spring summer fall winter

There are four seasons.
They happen in the same order each year.

How do the seasons change?

winter

Spring can be warm.
Summer can be hot.
Fall can be cool.
Winter can be cold.

Draw Different Kinds of Weather

Ask children to draw a picture of any kind of weather. Have them take turns showing their pictures to the rest of the class. Ask children to state sentences that describe the weather shown in their pictures. Record their sentences on the board. Challenge children to identify the season the weather may depict.

Sequence the Seasons

Have children explain the repeating pattern of seasons by copying and completing the following sentences.

_____ comes after winter.

_____ comes after spring.

_____ comes after summer.

_____ comes after fall.

Vocabulary

cloudy	sunny
fall	thermometer
rainy	weather
snowy	windsock
spring	windy
summer	winter